AM I T CHRIST LIKE?

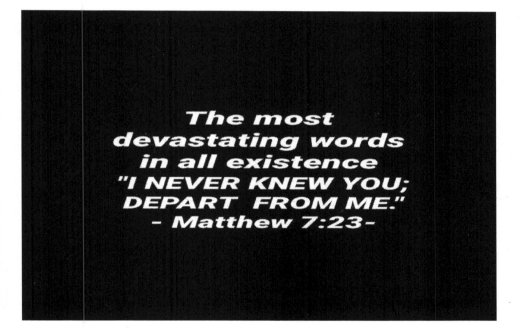

The most devastating words in all existence "I NEVER KNEW YOU; DEPART FROM ME." - Matthew 7:23-

To Be Christ Like, Is to Have Christ like behaviors.

By

Latasha L. Willingham

This book is dedicated to:

My wonderful and supportive husband Freeman. We have gone through this journey ogether experiencing things we planned and looked forward to in life and many things we did ot foresee for our lives but we pushed through together. I also must make a special dedication o our beautiful children, Tyanna, Duane, Breyanna and Jajuan whom I love so very much as hey bring so much joy into my life.

My mother Tijuana J. Warren for birthing me and acknowledging she knew nothing bout raising a baby and gave me back to GOD when I was born. My Grandparents Roosevelt & rances that stood in the gap raising me alongside my mom. My Dad Charles Staples for being here to stand in the gap when my biological Father was not.

My entire family and friends that remained by my side no matter what, when I needed hem most. There are too many to name but I pray that they know how much they all mean to me y the way I treat them.

The memory of my Grandparents Roosevelt & Frances Jackson, George Warren and izzie May Jones as well as my Great-Grandparents Pearl and Linual Yarbrough, my Great Aunt lorestine Tanzy, Uncle John 'Broach" Yarbrough & Uncle Albert Keith Warren all whom I ove dearly.

Those of us that are Believers in Christ that strive daily to live a true life in the Body of Christ. Although we are human being that are born sinners. We must truly be born again and by loing so we must look at our behaviors that we have been accustomed to. We often times falsely believe that our flesh does not over take us having us spiritually blind and not truly walking in he will of God.

Table of Contents

Introduction

Congratulations on taking a big step seeking the truth about yourself as you walk out your journey on this side of life. I decided to write Am I truly Christ like being a woman that is just like everyone else living a normal life as a wife, mother and a career woman is more than just what I desire but it is who the Lord desires for my life. After the back to back deaths of three of my closest family members and bad car accident of my own July of this year 2019 is what pushed me to complete this of three books I've been writing for some time now.

Once I truly surrendered to God and gave my whole life to Christ striving to be Christ like as a servant on the battlefield for the Lord, I changed how I viewed everything.

I learned the true power of God when he moved me from a situation not being really being involved in church, but I knew to ask and He did deliver me.

This book is to help each and every reader really look deep within self for errors that may or may not be Christ like that need correcting. Often times we are looking at others and their errors that we do not see our own. We also attempt to justify our errors to satisfy ourselves but this only hurts ourselves even more. We must take off our blinders to self-behaviors in order to correct them to truly walk in the will of the Lord. We too often look at what we look at as small verses large issues and this is why we are failing in the Body of Christ.

Being a woman chosen by God to preach His Word is both rewarding and challenging. It is rewarding knowing that I am one that God birthed into this world to stand out by speaking and teaching His true Word and most importantly to live my life by His true Word. I have been a part of so many things both good and not so good in the ministry. It was much easier for me before I accepted the call from God into the ministry because I only had to focus on my own family life. Being called by God requires so much more and I am thankful to God for creating me for this journey even through the times I wanted to throw in the towel.

Being in the Body of Christ is the most beneficial families in life. There is so much to this family that we take for granted. I want this book to be a guide to everyday life as we go through our journey. There are some things that we feel are not so bad but could most definitely cause us to hear those most devastating words "I NEVER KNEW YOU; DEPART FROM ME.'

We are missing the mark. Every day we see in the news how we as believers are allowing the enemy to consume us placing a dark cloud over the church. We, the believer are the church. We are committing horrible acts such as child molesting, adultery, homosexuality, lying, stealing, selfishness, hypocrisy and it goes on and on, right there in the House of the Lord.

When you read this small book you just may learn you too are committing horrible acts right in your own house of Worship, your own home and in your dealings with others.

It does not matter how long you've gone to church in your life. It does not matter how much money you make. It does not matter the type of vehicles you drive. It does not matter what type of house you live in. It does not matter about the color of your skin. It does not matter how much education you have. It does not matter if you are a Preacher Deacon or Pastor. We must be right and treat one another right. Honestly we all want to hear something like this for the Lord "WELL DONE, GOOD AND FAITHFUL SERVANT."

Chapter One: Why Did JESUS Have To Come In Human Form

Genesis Chapter 3 explains the fall of man. Due to the sin of Adam is why the JESUS CHRIST came to set us free from sin.

The serpent was clever, more clever than any wild animal GOD had made. He spoke to the Woman: "Do I understand that God told you not to eat from any tree in the garden?"

The Woman said to the serpent, "Not at all. We can eat from the trees in the garden. It's only about the tree in the middle of the garden that God said, 'Don't eat from it; don't even touch it or you'll die.'"

The serpent told the Woman, "You won't die. God knows that the moment you eat from that tree, you'll see what's really going on. You'll be just like God, knowing everything, ranging all the way from good to evil."

When the Woman saw that the tree looked like good eating and realized what she would get out of it—she'd know everything!—she took and ate the fruit and then gave some to her husband, and he ate.

Immediately the two of them did "see what's really going on"—saw themselves naked! They sewed fig leaves together as makeshift clothes for themselves.

When they heard the sound of GOD strolling in the garden in the evening breeze, the Man and his Wife hid in the trees of the garden, hid from GOD.

GOD called to the Man: "Where are you?"

He said, "I heard you in the garden and I was afraid because I was naked. And I hid."

GOD said, "Who told you you were naked? Did you eat from that tree I told you not to eat from?"

The Man said, "The Woman you gave me as a companion, she gave me fruit from the tree, and, yes, I ate it."

GOD said to the Woman, "What is this that you've done?" "The serpent seduced me," she said, "and I ate." GOD told the serpent:

'Because you've done this, you're cursed, cursed beyond all cattle animals
Cursed to slink on your belly and eat dirt all your life. I'm declaring war you and the Woman, between your offspring and hers. He'll wound your hea you'll wound his heel."

He told the Woman: "I'll multiply your pains in childbirth; you'll give birth to your babies in pain. You'll want to please your husband, but he'll lord it over you."

He told the Man: "Because you listened to your wife and ate from the tree That I commanded you not to eat from, 'Don't eat from this tree,' The very ground is cursed because of you; getting food from the ground Will be as painful as having babies is for your wife; you'll be working in pain all your life long. The ground will sprout thorns and weeds, you'll get your food the hard way, Planting and tilling and harvesting, sweating in the fields from dawn to dusk, Until you return to that ground yourself, dead and buried; you started out as dirt, you'll end up dirt."

The Man, known as Adam, named his wife Eve because she was the mother of all the living. GOD made leather clothing for Adam and his wife and dressed them.

GOD said, "The Man has become like one of us, capable of knowing everything, ranging from good to evil. What if he now should reach out and take fruit from the Tree-of-Life and eat, and live forever? Never—this cannot happen!"

So GOD expelled them from the Garden of Eden and sent them to work the ground, the same dirt out of which they'd been made. He threw them out of the garden and stationed angel-cherubim and a revolving sword of fire east of it, guarding the path to the Tree-of-Life.

Now, this should give us a better understanding of what happened in the beginning of us being dead in sin. We are all born with sinful natures and this is why Jesus had to come giving us the only way out of sin. Later we will understand more about being born again and why it is so important for us to do so. Being born again a renewed life in CHRIST and is the key to truly being CHRIST LIKE.

-Giving Gift-(Romans 5:14-17)

ım landed us in the dilemma we're in—first sin,
:rom either sin or death. That sin disturbed relations
:ryone, but the extent of the disturbance was not
. detail to Moses. So death, this huge abyss
ıated the landscape from Adam to Moses. Even
as Adam did by disobeying a specific command of
God still had ~ ~ .s termination of life, this separation from God. But
Adam, who got us into this, also points ahead to the One who will get us out of it.

Yet the rescuing gift is not exactly parallel to the death-dealing sin. If one man's
sin put crowds of people at the dead-end abyss of separation from God, just think
what God's gift poured through one man, Jesus Christ, will do! There's no
comparison between that death-dealing sin and this generous, life-giving gift. The
verdict on that one sin was the death sentence; the verdict on the many sins that
followed was this wonderful life sentence. If death got the upper hand through one
man's wrongdoing, can you imagine the breathtaking recovery life makes,
sovereign life, in those who grasp with both hands this wildly extravagant life-gift,
this grand setting-everything-right, that the one man Jesus Christ provides?

SELF EVALUATION TIME

After reading how the sin of man began, doesn't this seem familiar as we
live our daily lives? Isn't there always something or someone that attempts to
make a wrong look right? The serpent approached the woman with going against
Gods instructions. She then chooses to do it. Once she does it, she then approach
her husband to go against Gods instructions. Adam, the one that God gave the
initial instruction to in the first place choose to go against God and this is when it
all went from bad to worst.

Notice I use the words "CHOSE/CHOOSE" everything from then to now is
a choice. Just as Adam and Eve knew what they were instructed to and not to do,
we do as well. Although the serpent only threw it out for them to do, it was not
until they themselves chose to go against Gods will when they were punished. We
too must know that it is Gods instructions that we go against when we choose to do
wrong not matter how much good we may feel about it. I know for myself, I am a

4

ery defensive person and I will fly off the handle when someone does something hat hurts me or simply pisses me off but I also understand clearly, I am going gainst what the Lord expects from me and I have no one to blame but myself. We ll have something(s) that pushes us but in order to stay in the Will of God we nust push that much more to do better. Yes, we are able to be forgiven because ve are not perfect people but often times we do things expecting forgiveness from Jod when we should have more expectations for ourselves to do the right things in he first place.

It is so easy for us to convince ourselves our wrongs are justified for our own benefits but we must understand we are not going against our own nstructions, these are Gods instructions that we are not lining ourselves up with. So ask yourself, is it most beneficial to please my own feelings or to be out of the Vill of God?

Often times we falsely convince ourselves that we are so much better than others. We as people must understand that not one us are any better than the next person, we just do things differently. We just look differently. When it comes to being better it must be in our behaviors by being a better person by doing what's right according to Gods will, not our will. I stress this because there was/is not one person that could do what Christ did because we are all in the flesh and we have he exact same sinful nature as Adam and Eve. This was the beginning of sin but because God loves us so much He would not leave us dead and in this same sinful ituation without a way out. We have our way out of sin because His SON came both divine and human as He walked the face of this earth until the day He died vith each and every sin we have and will commit.

Christ had to come down from Heaven because He was/is the only one that's sinless. This is why the Holy Spirit came upon a virgin woman by the name of Mary placing the Holy Seed of Christ to be birthed. Therefore, no one have any authentic reason to believe we are more than anyone else. Material items is not what defy us to GOD and this is what we get confused in our perceptions of who is worthy and who is not worthy. This is a life threatening mistake for us all!

SELF EVALUATION TIME

How do you look at others? How do you fall in this category of thinking you are better than someone else? Your clothing, degrees, symbols on the vehicles you drive, bank statements, position on your job, position in the church, color of your skin, the sin someone else commit are worse than yours, according to you?

No one have the right to brag about being better when only CHRIST is the one that walked the face of this earth Holy and sinless!

You can be in church every day but you will still never be Holier than the next person. We must sincerely understand this and not just say, "oh I know I am not any better than the next person" but the your true actions and attitude proves it most often and people see it more than you realize you reveal it! This issue will be in more detail later in the book in more detail.

List things I can do better according to the scriptures I read in this chapter

_____
_____
_____
_____
_____
_____
_____

List of things I am not proud about that I am going to ask god to help me correct

_____
_____
_____
_____
_____
_____

Things that I am thankful to say I do well to build up the body of Christ

_____
_____
_____
_____
_____
_____

JESUS came to do the Will of our Father in Heaven.

Jesus said, "I am the Bread of Life. The person who aligns with me hungers no more and thirsts no more, ever. I have told you this explicitly because even though you have seen me in action, you don't really believe me. Every person the Father gives me eventually comes running to me. And once that person is with me, I hold on and don't let go. I came down from heaven not to follow my own whim but to accomplish the will of the One who sent me.

JESUS came to save us sinners. Only JESUS, being sinless was/is the answer for each and every one of us the chance to receive eternal life with GOD.

Here's a word you can take to heart and depend on: Jesus Christ came into the world to save sinners. I'm proof—Public Sinner Number One—of someone who could never have made it apart from sheer mercy. And now he shows me off—evidence of his endless patience—to those who are right on the edge of trusting him forever.

JESUS came bear witness to the truth

Then Pilate said, "So, are you a king or not?" Jesus answered, "You tell me. Because I am King, I was born and entered the world so that I could witness to the truth. Everyone who cares for truth, who has any feeling for the truth, recognizes my voice."

JESUS came to give light (life) into this dark (dead) world

Whoever makes a practice of sinning is of the devil, for the devil has been sinning from the beginning. The reason the Son of God appeared was to destroy the works of the devil.

If I had not come and spoken to them, they would not have been guilty of sin, but now they have no excuse for their sin.

JESUS came to feel what we feel as people

Since therefore the children share in flesh and blood, he himself likewise partook of the same things, that through death he might destroy the one who has the power of death, that is, the devil, and deliver all those who through fear of death were subject to lifelong slavery. For surely it is not angels that he helps, but e helps the offspring of Abraham. Therefore he had to be made like his brothers in every respect, so that he might become a merciful and faithful high priest in the service of God, to make propitiation for the sins of the people.

JESUS came to seek and save the lost

And when Jesus came to the place, he looked up and said to him, "Zacchaeus, hurry and come down, for I must stay at your house today." So he hurried and came down and received him joyfully. And when they saw it, they all grumbled, "He has gone in to be the guest of a man who is a sinner." And Zacchaeus stood and said to the Lord, "Behold, Lord, the half of my goods I give to the poor. And if have defrauded anyone of anything, I restore it fourfold." And Jesus said to him, "Today salvation has come to this house, since he also is a son of Abraham. For the Son of Man came to seek and to save the lost."

JESUS came to reveal the Father's Glory and Love for His people

And the Word became flesh and dwelt among us, and we have seen his glory, glory as of the only Son from the Father, full of grace and truth.

JESUS came to give us the chance at Eternal Life

"I'm telling you the most solemn and sober truth now: Whoever believes in me has real life, eternal life. I am the Bread of Life. Your ancestors ate the manna bread in the desert and died. But now here is Bread that truly comes down out of heaven. Anyone eating this Bread will not die, ever. I am the Bread—living Bread!—who came down out of heaven. Anyone who eats this Bread will live—and forever! The Bread that I present to the world so that it can eat and live is myself, this flesh-and-blood self."

Chapter Two: The Examples of Characteristics JESUS CHRIST left us

It goes without saying that JESUS gave the ultimate example of Love by giving His life for us. This chapter will show the actual Characteristics JESUS showed during His time here on earth. JESUS walked with such humility while here in human form. It brings such great emotions of joy and thanksgiving as I write this just thinking of how we are so loved that the SON of GOD our big brother and Savior would feel and exemplify each and every emotion we as people feel.

What an awesome GOD we serve to not just give instructions but to live out the instructions Himself. This is why we are blessed with so much patience from our Father as the SON is on the right side of the throne pleading our cases as He knows first hand the difficulty of living on this side of life! This is why we must look within ourselves and line up with CHRIST like living as He gave His all for us to have a change, if only we choose to be obedient.

Jesus took time to really listen to people and what they were saying and felt. His responses were always thoughtful not just wanting people to shut up for him to say what he wanted to say. We as people so often hear a person speaking but only wanting to say what we want to say, therefore not really being thoughtful of what the other person is truly feeling and saying. This is one of the greatest reasons why we don't change our behaviors because we choose not to really understand other ways of thinking and behaving.

Jesus exemplified compassion for people especially those that felt helpless and hopeless. Those that most people looked down on Jesus lifted them up. Jesus shows us that time and time again we are no greater or less than anyone. Here we are talking about how our Lord and Savior walked among the people in the world just like we all walk around and go about our daily lives. The only difference is too often we that are not sinless treat one another as if we are the Lord with our nasty attitudes looking down on one another.

Jesus showed compassion for the sick, those that were treated differently because of social injustice, those that were possessed by demonic spirits, those that were outcasts according to the people, to name a few.

One day in one of the villages there was a man covered with leprosy. When he saw Jesus he fell down before him in prayer and said, "If you want to, you can leanse me." Jesus put out his hand, touched him, and said, "I want to. Be clean." Then and there his skin was smooth, the leprosy gone. Jesus instructed him, "Don't talk about this all over town. Just quietly present your healed self to the priest, along with the offering ordered by Moses. Your cleansed and obedient life, not your words, will bear witness to what I have done." But the man couldn't keep it to himself, and the word got out. Soon a large crowd of people had gathered to listen and be healed of their ailments. As often as possible Jesus withdrew to out-of-the-way places for prayer.

Jesus exemplified respect for people, those that were poor, hopeless and mistreated by those in power. Jesus showed great respect for women and children. Jesus would not be very calm when the Holy temple of GOD was defiled and when dealing with the religious hypocrites, and even then he would show restraint.

He came to Nazareth where he had been reared. As he always did on the Sabbath, he went to the meeting place. When he stood up to read, he was handed the scroll of the prophet Isaiah. Unrolling the scroll, he found the place where it was written, God's Spirit is on me; he's chosen me to preach the Message of good news to the poor, Sent me to announce pardon to prisoners and recovery of sight to the blind, To set the burdened and battered free, to announce, "This is God's year to act!"

He rolled up the scroll, handed it back to the assistant, and sat down. Every eye in the place was on him, intent. Then he started in, "You've just heard Scripture make history. It came true just now in this place."

He was teaching in one of the meeting places on the Sabbath. There was a woman present, so twisted and bent over with arthritis that she couldn't even look up. She had been afflicted with this for eighteen years. When Jesus saw her, he called her over. "Woman, you're free!" He laid hands on her and suddenly she was standing straight and tall, giving glory to God. The meeting-place president, furious because Jesus had healed on the Sabbath, said to the congregation, "Six days have been defined as work days. Come on one of the six if you want to be healed, but not on the seventh, the Sabbath." But Jesus shot back, "You frauds! Each Sabbath every one of you regularly unties your cow or donkey from its stall, leads it out for water, and thinks nothing of it. So why isn't it all right for me to untie this daughter of Abraham and lead her from the stall where Satan has had her tied these eighteen years?" When he put it that way, his critics were left looking quite silly and red-faced. The congregation was delighted and cheered him on.

11

The people brought children to Jesus, hoping he might touch them. The disciples shooed them off. But Jesus was irate and let them know it: "Don't push these children away. Don't ever get between them and me. These children are at the very center of life in the kingdom. Mark this: Unless you accept God's kingdom in the simplicity of a child, you'll never get in." Then, gathering the children up in his arms, he laid his hands of blessing on them.

Jesus was such a kind and gentle person He never looked to belittle anyone He showed the greatest example of what we are to be as servers of others. When Jesus washed the feet of His disciples this is where we as people really miss the mark. We like to feel as if we show our greatness by the service of others doing things for us when Jesus clearly exemplified the opposite of greatness by washing the feet of the disciples. Being great is not about royal treatment towards yourself when Jesus Christ our Lord and Savior gave us this example.

Jesus taught us to be selfless not selfish, humble not arrogant. Everything is not always about us on the receiving end. When we are blessed enough to bless someone else this is what we are to do. Here we are seeing God himself washing his Disciples feet but we have the nerve to believe we are only at our best when someone is serving us.

Then he said, "Do you understand what I have done to you? You address me as 'Teacher' and 'Master,' and rightly so. That is what I am. So if I, the Master and Teacher, washed your feet, you must now wash each other's feet. I've laid down a pattern for you. What I've done, you do. I'm only pointing out the obvious. A servant is not ranked above his master; an employee doesn't give orders to the employer. If you understand what I'm telling you, act like it—and live a blessed life.

If you've gotten anything at all out of following Christ, if his love has made any difference in your life, if being in a community of the Spirit means anything to you, if you have a heart, if you care— then do me a favor: Agree with each other, love each other, be deep-spirited friends. Don't push your way to the front; don't sweet-talk your way to the top. Put yourself aside, and help others get ahead. Don't be obsessed with getting your own advantage. Forget yourselves long enough to lend a helping hand.

Think of yourselves the way Christ Jesus thought of himself. He had equal status with God but didn't think so much of himself that he had to cling to the advantages of that status no matter what. Not at all. When the time came, he set aside the privileges of deity and took on the status of a slave, became human! Having become human, he stayed human. It was an incredibly humbling process. He didn't claim special privileges. Instead, he lived a selfless, obedient life and then died a selfless, obedient death—and the worst kind of death at that—a crucifixion.

Jesus exemplified Sacrifice and Forgiveness in a way no one can doubt or duplicate. Jesus came down from heaven feeling all the emotions we as people do. Jesus felt rejection, temptation, betrayal, loneliness, disappointments, pain. Jesus felt everything we feel and go through.

Next Jesus was taken into the wild by the Spirit for the Test. The Devil was ready to give it. Jesus prepared for the Test by fasting forty days and forty nights. That left him, of course, in a state of extreme hunger, which the Devil took advantage of in the first test: "Since you are God's Son, speak the word that will turn these stones into loaves of bread."

Jesus answered by quoting Deuteronomy: "It takes more than bread to stay alive. It takes a steady stream of words from God's mouth."

For the second test the Devil took him to the Holy City. He sat him on top of the Temple and said, "Since you are God's Son, jump." The Devil goaded him by quoting Psalm 91: "He has placed you in the care of angels. They will catch you so that you won't so much as stub your toe on a stone."

Jesus countered with another citation from Deuteronomy: "Don't you dare test the Lord your God."

For the third test, the Devil took him to the peak of a huge mountain. He gestured expansively, pointing out all the earth's kingdoms, how glorious they all were. Then he said, "They're yours—lock, stock, and barrel. Just go down on your knees and worship me, and they're yours."

Jesus' refusal was curt: "Beat it, Satan!" He backed his rebuke with a third quotation from Deuteronomy: "Worship the Lord your God, and only him. Serve him with absolute single-heartedness."

The Test was over. The Devil left. And in his place, angels! Angels came and took care of Jesus' needs.

13

JESUS ULTIMATE EXAMPLE OF LOVE AND SACRIFICE

"This is how much God loved the world: He gave his Son, his one and only Son. And this is why: so that no one need be destroyed; by believing in him, anyone can have a whole and lasting life. God didn't go to all the trouble of sending his Son merely to point an accusing finger, telling the world how bad it was. He came to help, to put the world right again. Anyone who trusts in him is acquitted; anyone who refuses to trust him has long since been under the death sentence without knowing it. And why? Because of that person's failure to believe in the one-of-a-kind Son of God when introduced to him.

Jesus, having prayed this prayer, left with his disciples and crossed over the brook Kidron at a place where there was a garden. He and his disciples entered it.

Judas, his betrayer, knew the place because Jesus and his disciples went there often. So Judas led the way to the garden, and the Roman soldiers and police sent by the high priests and Pharisees followed. They arrived there with lanterns and torches and swords. Jesus, knowing by now everything that was coming down on him, went out and met them. He said, "Who are you after?"

They answered, "Jesus the Nazarene."

He said, "That's me." The soldiers recoiled, totally taken aback. Judas, his betrayer, stood out like a sore thumb.

Jesus asked again, "Who are you after?"

They answered, "Jesus the Nazarene."

"I told you," said Jesus, "that's me. I'm the one. So if it's me you're after, let these others go." (This validated the words in his prayer, "I didn't lose one of those you gave.")

Just then Simon Peter, who was carrying a sword, pulled it from its sheath and struck the Chief Priest's servant, cutting off his right ear. Malchus was the servant's name.

Jesus ordered Peter, "Put back your sword. Do you think for a minute I'm not going to drink this cup the Father gave me?"

Then the Roman soldiers under their commander, joined by the Jewish police, seized Jesus and tied him up. They took him first to Annas, father-in-law of

14

Caiaphas. Caiaphas was the Chief Priest that year. It was Caiaphas who had advised the Jews that it was to their advantage that one man die for the people.

Simon Peter and another disciple followed Jesus. That other disciple was known to the Chief Priest, and so he went in with Jesus to the Chief Priest's courtyard. Peter had to stay outside. Then the other disciple went out, spoke to the doorkeeper, and got Peter in.

The young woman who was the doorkeeper said to Peter, "Aren't you one of this man's disciples?"

He said, "No, I'm not."

The servants and police had made a fire because of the cold and were huddled there warming themselves. Peter stood with them, trying to get warm.

The Interrogation

Annas interrogated Jesus regarding his disciples and his teaching. Jesus answered, "I've spoken openly in public. I've taught regularly in meeting places and the Temple, where the Jews all come together. Everything has been out in the open. I've said nothing in secret. So why are you treating me like a conspirator? Question those who have been listening to me. They know well what I have said. My teachings have all been aboveboard."

When he said this, one of the policemen standing there slapped Jesus across the face, saying, "How dare you speak to the Chief Priest like that!"

Jesus replied, "If I've said something wrong, prove it. But if I've spoken the plain truth, why this slapping around?"

Then Annas sent him, still tied up, to the Chief Priest Caiaphas.

Meanwhile, Simon Peter was back at the fire, still trying to get warm. The others there said to him, "Aren't you one of his disciples?"

He denied it, "Not me."

One of the Chief Priest's servants, a relative of the man whose ear Peter had cut off, said, "Didn't I see you in the garden with him?"

Again, Peter denied it. Just then a rooster crowed.

The King of the Jews

They led Jesus then from Caiaphas to the Roman governor's palace. It was early morning. They themselves didn't enter the palace because they didn't want to be disqualified from eating the Passover. So Pilate came out to them and spoke. "What charge do you bring against this man?"

They said, "If he hadn't been doing something evil, do you think we'd be here bothering you?"

Pilate said, "You take him. Judge him by your law."

The Jews said, "We're not allowed to kill anyone." (This would confirm Jesus' word indicating the way he would die.)

Pilate went back into the palace and called for Jesus. He said, "Are you the 'King of the Jews'?"

Jesus answered, "Are you saying this on your own, or did others tell you this about me?"

Pilate said, "Do I look like a Jew? Your people and your high priests turned you over to me. What did you do?"

"My kingdom," said Jesus, "doesn't consist of what you see around you. If it did, my followers would fight so that I wouldn't be handed over to the Jews. But I'm not that kind of king, not the world's kind of king."

Then Pilate said, "So, are you a king or not?"

Jesus answered, "You tell me. Because I am King, I was born and entered the world so that I could witness to the truth. Everyone who cares for truth, who has any feeling for the truth, recognizes my voice."

Pilate said, "What is truth?"

Then he went back out to the Jews and told them, "I find nothing wrong in this man. It's your custom that I pardon one prisoner at Passover. Do you want me to pardon the 'King of the Jews'?"

They shouted back, "Not this one, but Barabbas!" Barabbas was a Jewish freedom fighter.

The Thorn Crown of the King

So Pilate took Jesus and had him whipped. The soldiers, having braided a crown from thorns, set it on his head, threw a purple robe over him, and approached him with, "Hail, King of the Jews!" Then they greeted him with slaps in the face.

Pilate went back out again and said to them, "I present him to you, but I want you to know that I do not find him guilty of any crime." Just then Jesus came out wearing the thorn crown and purple robe.

Pilate announced, "Here he is: the Man."

When the high priests and police saw him, they shouted in a frenzy, "Crucify! Crucify!"

Pilate told them, "You take him. You crucify him. I find nothing wrong with him."

The Jews answered, "We have a law, and by that law he must die because he claimed to be the Son of God."

When Pilate heard this, he became even more scared. He went back into the palace and said to Jesus, "Where did you come from?"Jesus gave no answer.

Pilate said, "You won't talk? Don't you know that I have the authority to pardon you, and the authority to—crucify you?"

Jesus said, "You haven't a shred of authority over me except what has been given you from heaven. That's why the one who betrayed me to you has committed a far greater fault."

At this, Pilate tried his best to pardon him, but the Jews shouted him down: "If you pardon this man, you're no friend of Caesar's. Anyone setting himself up as 'king' defies Caesar."

When Pilate heard those words, he led Jesus outside. He sat down at the judgment seat in the area designated Stone Court (in Hebrew, Gabbatha). It was the preparation day for Passover. The hour was noon. Pilate said to the Jews, "Here is your king."

They shouted back, "Kill him! Kill him! Crucify him!"

Pilate said, "I am to crucify your king?"

The high priests answered, "We have no king except Caesar."

Pilate caved in to their demand. He turned him over to be crucified.

The Crucifixion

They took Jesus away. Carrying his cross, Jesus went out to the place called Skull Hill (the name in Hebrew is Golgotha), where they crucified him, and with him two others, one on each side, Jesus in the middle. Pilate wrote a sign and had it placed on the cross. It read:

jesus the nazarene the king of the jews.

Many of the Jews read the sign because the place where Jesus was crucified was right next to the city. It was written in Hebrew, Latin, and Greek. The Jewish high priests objected. "Don't write," they said to Pilate, "'The King of the Jews.' Make it, 'This man said, "I am the King of the Jews."'"

Pilate said, "What I've written, I've written."

When they crucified him, the Roman soldiers took his clothes and divided them up four ways, to each soldier a fourth. But his robe was seamless, a single piece of weaving, so they said to each other, "Let's not tear it up. Let's throw dice to see who gets it." This confirmed the Scripture that said, "They divided up my clothes among them and threw dice for my coat." (The soldiers validated the Scriptures!)

While the soldiers were looking after themselves, Jesus' mother, his aunt, Mary the wife of Clopas, and Mary Magdalene stood at the foot of the cross. Jesus saw his mother and the disciple he loved standing near her. He said to his mother, "Woman, here is your son." Then to the disciple, "Here is your mother." From that moment the disciple accepted her as his own mother.

Jesus, seeing that everything had been completed so that the Scripture record might also be complete, then said, "I'm thirsty."

A jug of sour wine was standing by. Someone put a sponge soaked with the wine on a javelin and lifted it to his mouth. After he took the wine, Jesus said, "It's done . . . complete." Bowing his head, he offered up his spirit.

Then the Jews, since it was the day of Sabbath preparation, and so the bodies wouldn't stay on the crosses over the Sabbath (it was a high holy day that year), petitioned Pilate that their legs be broken to speed death, and the bodies taken down. So the soldiers came and broke the legs of the first man crucified with Jesus, and then the other. When they got to Jesus, they saw that he was already dead, so they didn't break his legs. One of the soldiers stabbed him in the side with his spear. Blood and water gushed out.

The eyewitness to these things has presented an accurate report. He saw it himself and is telling the truth so that you, also, will believe.

These things that happened confirmed the Scripture, "Not a bone in his body was broken," and the other Scripture that reads, "They will stare at the one they pierced."

After all this, Joseph of Arimathea (he was a disciple of Jesus, but secretly, because he was intimidated by the Jews) petitioned Pilate to take the body of Jesus. Pilate gave permission. So Joseph came and took the body.

Nicodemus, who had first come to Jesus at night, came now in broad daylight carrying a mixture of myrrh and aloes, about seventy-five pounds. They took Jesus' body and, following the Jewish burial custom, wrapped it in linen with the spices. There was a garden near the place he was crucified, and in the garden a new tomb in which no one had yet been placed. So, because it was Sabbath preparation for the Jews and the tomb was convenient, they placed Jesus in it.

Resurrection!

Early in the morning on the first day of the week, while it was still dark, Mary Magdalene came to the tomb and saw that the stone was moved away from the entrance. She ran at once to Simon Peter and the other disciple, the one Jesus loved, breathlessly panting, "They took the Master from the tomb. We don't know where they've put him."

Peter and the other disciple left immediately for the tomb. They ran, neck and neck. The other disciple got to the tomb first, outrunning Peter. Stooping to look in, he saw the pieces of linen cloth lying there, but he didn't go in. Simon Peter arrived after him, entered the tomb, observed the linen cloths lying there, and the kerchief used to cover his head not lying with the linen cloths but separate, neatly folded by itself. Then the other disciple, the one who had gotten there first, went into the tomb, took one look at the evidence, and believed. No one yet knew from the Scripture that he had to rise from the dead. The disciples then went back home.

But Mary stood outside the tomb weeping. As she wept, she knelt to look into the tomb and saw two angels sitting there, dressed in white, one at the head, the other at the foot of where Jesus' body had been laid. They said to her, "Woman, why do you weep?"

"They took my Master," she said, "and I don't know where they put him." After she said this, she turned away and saw Jesus standing there. But she didn't recognize him.

Jesus spoke to her, "Woman, why do you weep? Who are you looking for?"

She, thinking that he was the gardener, said, "Mister, if you took him, tell me where you put him so I can care for him."

Jesus said, "Mary."

Turning to face him, she said in Hebrew, "Rabboni!" meaning "Teacher!"

Jesus said, "Don't cling to me, for I have not yet ascended to the Father. Go to my brothers and tell them, 'I ascend to my Father and your Father, my God and your God.'"

Mary Magdalene went, telling the news to the disciples: "I saw the Master!" And she told them everything he said to her.

To Believe

Later on that day, the disciples had gathered together, but, fearful of the Jews, had locked all the doors in the house. Jesus entered, stood among them, and said, "Peace to you." Then he showed them his hands and side.

The disciples, seeing the Master with their own eyes, were exuberant. Jesus repeated his greeting: "Peace to you. Just as the Father sent me, I send you."

Then he took a deep breath and breathed into them. "Receive the Holy Spirit," he said. "If you forgive someone's sins, they're gone for good. If you don't forgive sins, what are you going to do with them?"

But Thomas, sometimes called the Twin, one of the Twelve, was not with them when Jesus came. The other disciples told him, "We saw the Master."

But he said, "Unless I see the nail holes in his hands, put my finger in the nail holes, and stick my hand in his side, I won't believe it." Eight days later, his disciples were again in the room. This time Thomas was with them. Jesus came through the locked doors, stood among them, and said, "Peace to you."

Then he focused his attention on Thomas. "Take your finger and examine my hands. Take your hand and stick it in my side. Don't be unbelieving. Believe."

Thomas said, "My Master! My God!"

Jesus said, "So, you believe because you've seen with your own eyes. Even better blessings are in store for those who believe without seeing."

Jesus provided far more God-revealing signs than are written down in this book. These are written down so you will believe that Jesus is the Messiah, the Son of God, and in the act of believing, have real and eternal life in the way he personally revealed it.

Chapter Three: How Did The Church Get Built And Why

When Jesus arrived in the villages of Caesarea Philippi, he asked his disciples, "What are people saying about who the Son of Man is?"

They replied, "Some think he is John the Baptizer, some say Elijah, some Jeremiah or one of the other prophets."

He pressed them, "And how about you? Who do you say I am?"

Simon Peter said, "You're the Christ, the Messiah, the Son of the living God."

Jesus came back, "God bless you, Simon, son of Jonah! You didn't get that answer out of books or from teachers. My Father in heaven, God himself, let you in on this secret of who I really am. And now I'm going to tell you who you are, really are. You are Peter, a rock. This is the rock on which I will put together my church, a church so expansive with energy that not even the gates of hell will be able to keep it out.

"And that's not all. You will have complete and free access to God's kingdom, keys to open any and every door: no more barriers between heaven and earth, earth and heaven. A yes on earth is yes in heaven. A no on earth is no in heaven."

He swore the disciples to secrecy. He made them promise they would tell no one that he was the Messiah.

Risen from the Dead

After the Sabbath, as the first light of the new week dawned, Mary Magdalene and the other Mary came to keep vigil at the tomb. Suddenly the earth reeled and rocked under their feet as God's angel came down from heaven, came right up to where they were standing. He rolled back the stone and then sat on it. Shafts of lightning blazed from him. His garments shimmered snow-white. The guards at the tomb were scared to death. They were so frightened, they couldn't move.

The angel spoke to the women: "There is nothing to fear here. I know you're looking for Jesus, the One they nailed to the cross. He is not here. He was raised, just as he said. Come and look at the place where he was placed.

"Now, get on your way quickly and tell his disciples, 'He is risen from the dead. He is going on ahead of you to Galilee. You will see him there.' That's the message."

The women, deep in wonder and full of joy, lost no time in leaving the tomb. They ran to tell the disciples. Then Jesus met them, stopping them in their tracks. "Good morning!" he said. They fell to their knees, embraced his feet, and worshiped him. Jesus said, "You're holding on to me for dear life! Don't be frightened like that. Go tell my brothers that they are to go to Galilee, and that I'll meet them there."

Meanwhile, the guards had scattered, but a few of them went into the city and told the high priests everything that had happened. They called a meeting of the religious leaders and came up with a plan: They took a large sum of money and gave it to the soldiers, bribing them to say, "His disciples came in the night and stole the body while we were sleeping." They assured them, "If the governor hears about your sleeping on duty, we will make sure you don't get blamed." The soldiers took the bribe and did as they were told. That story, cooked up in the Jewish High Council, is still going around.

Meanwhile, the eleven disciples were on their way to Galilee, headed for the mountain Jesus had set for their reunion. The moment they saw him they worshiped him. Some, though, held back, not sure about worship, about risking themselves totally.

Jesus, undeterred, went right ahead and gave his charge: "God authorized and commanded me to commission you: Go out and train everyone you meet, far and near, in this way of life, marking them by baptism in the threefold name: Father, Son, and Holy Spirit. Then instruct them in the practice of all I have commanded you. I'll be with you as you do this, day after day after day, right up to the end of the age."

God didn't set us up for an angry rejection but for salvation by our Master, Jesus Christ. He died for us, a death that triggered life. Whether we're awake with the living or asleep with the dead, we're alive with him! So speak encouraging words to one another. Build up hope so you'll all be together in this, no one left out, no one left behind. I know you're already doing this; just keep on doing it.

The Full Assurance of Faith

Therefore, brothers, since we have confidence to enter the holy places by the blood of Jesus, by the new and living way that he opened for us through the curtain, that is, through his flesh, and since we have a great priest over the house of God, let us draw near with a true heart in full assurance of faith, with our hearts sprinkled clean from an evil conscience and our bodies washed with pure water.

Let us hold fast the confession of our hope without wavering, for he who promised is faithful. And let us consider how to stir up one another to love and good works, not neglecting to meet together, as is the habit of some, but encouraging one another, and all the more as you see the Day drawing near.

For if we go on sinning deliberately after receiving the knowledge of the truth, there no longer remains a sacrifice for sins, but a fearful expectation of judgment, and a fury of fire that will consume the adversaries. Anyone who has set aside the law of Moses dies without mercy on the evidence of two or three witnesses. How much worse punishment, do you think, will be deserved by the one who has trampled underfoot the Son of God, and has profaned the blood of the covenant by which he was sanctified, and has outraged the Spirit of grace? For we know him who said, "Vengeance is mine; I will repay." And again, "The Lord will judge his people." It is a fearful thing to fall into the hands of the living God.

But recall the former days when, after you were enlightened, you endured a hard struggle with sufferings, sometimes being publicly exposed to reproach and affliction, and sometimes being partners with those so treated. For you had compassion on those in prison, and you joyfully accepted the plundering of your property, since you knew that you yourselves had a better possession and an abiding one. Therefore do not throw away your confidence, which has a great reward. For you have need of endurance, so that when you have done the will of God you may receive what is promised. For, "Yet a little while, and the coming one will come and will not delay; but my righteous one shall live by faith, and if he shrinks back, my soul has no pleasure in him."But we are not of those who shrink back and are destroyed, but of those who have faith and preserve their souls.

For where two or three are gathered in my name, there am I among them.

SELF EVALUATION TIME

Now, that we see how the and why the church was built and why ask yourself is your service truly as it should be in the church.

I know for myself, I went to church just because I was doing it as a child. My grandfather took me to church where he served as a Sunday School teacher. I did like to go to church as we had a day care center in there, we often ate good and there were some nice people there.

Once I was an adult I went from time to time but honestly had this attitude that I did not need to go to church. I was a good person. I helped people when they needed me to. I knew who God and Jesus was.

Turns out I was spiritually blind. I did not have a relationship with the Lord meaning, I went to in the church building but that was it. I would usually, not pay attention to the message being delivered. I was often talking to someone that was around me. I am always honest about an issue I had with the preachers always saying the same ole thing every time I went to church. Turns out that was the best thing I could've heard and that was the actual Gospel of Jesus Christ. Jesus died, Jesus was buried, Jesus got out the grave in 3 days!

List things I can do better according to the scriptures I read in this chapter

_____
_____
_____
_____
_____
_____

List of things I am not proud about that I am going to ask god to help me correct

_____
_____
_____
_____
_____
_____

Things that I am thankful to say I do well to build up the body of Christ

_____
_____
_____
_____
_____
_____

Chapter Four: Exemplifying Characteristics Of CHRIST Living

So, chosen by God for this new life of love, dress in the wardrobe God picked out for you: compassion, kindness, humility, quiet strength, discipline. Be even-tempered, content with second place, quick to forgive an offense. Forgive as quickly and completely as the Master forgave you. And regardless of what else you put on, wear love. It's your basic, all-purpose garment. Never be without it.

If someone claims, "I know him well!" but doesn't keep his commandments, he's obviously a liar. His life doesn't match his words. But the one who keeps God's word is the person in whom we see God's mature love. This is the only way to be sure we're in God. Anyone who claims to be intimate with God ought to live the same kind of life Jesus lived.

This is the kind of life you've been invited into, the kind of life Christ lived. He suffered everything that came his way so you would know that it could be done, and also know how to do it, step-by-step.

He never did one thing wrong,

Not once said anything amiss.

They called him every name in the book and he said nothing back. He suffered in silence, content to let God set things right. He used his servant body to carry our sins to the Cross so we could be rid of sin, free to live the right way. His wounds became your healing. You were lost sheep with no idea who you were or where you were going. Now you're named and kept for good by the Shepherd of your souls.

It pleases me that you continue to remember and honor me by keeping up the traditions of the faith I taught you. All actual authority stems from Christ.

SELF EVALUATION TIME

I was living a normal life as a wife with our four children, a career in healthcare Management.

Although I claim to be just an average Joe type of person, I've always known there was much more to me that most could see physically. I went to church just as many all of my life. I went to church because that's just what I was accustomed to do out of habit since I was a little girl. I went mostly with my Grandfather that raised me. He was a true man of faith that kept me deep rooted in Jesus even though I didn't realize it.

I remember the day I accepted Christ as my Lord and Savior during Vacation Bible Study. I really didn't know what I was doing, I honestly did it just because I knew that was what I was expected to do. Yes, I knew Jesus, Yes, I believed in Jesus, but no, I did not really understand the benefits of accepting Christ as my Lord and Savior.

Now that I know what it is to have a sincere relationship with God, ill never turn away from this beautiful life. Often people say I will give my life to God when I get myself together. Well I have to let you know what I learned. YOU CANT GET RIGHT UNTIL YOU GIVE YOURSELF TO HIM FIRST!

We cant live a ratchet lifestyle and expect people to follow us to Christ. We cant be liars and whoremongers, thieves, adulterers, jealous hearted, gossipers and expect people to take us serious about being in the Lord, come on that is just insane but we get mad when people say we are fake. I feel the same way and this is why I must work to keep myself in line. No we are not perfect and by no means Jesus Himself, but it is time out for all these lame excuses as to why we continue to do wrong but expect folks to believe we are right. We would rather lie to ourselves that people are jealous of us because they are not fooled by our sneaky and lying ways. Especially those of us that are ministers, we are no better but we accepted to do better. Women ministers we already have it tough so don't make it worse by our actions that are certainly not lining up with the will of God.

List things I can do better according to the scriptures I read in this chapter

_____
_____
_____
_____
_____
_____
_____

List of things I am not proud about that I am going to ask god to help me correct

_____
_____
_____
_____
_____
_____
_____

Things that I am thankful to say I do well to build up the body of Christ

_____
_____
_____
_____
_____
_____
_____

Chapter Five: Our Dealings In The House Of The LORD

Leadership in the Church

If anyone wants to provide leadership in the church, good! But there are preconditions: A leader must be well-thought-of, committed to his wife, cool and collected, accessible, and hospitable. He must know what he's talking about, not be overfond of wine, not pushy but gentle, not thin-skinned, not money-hungry. He must handle his own affairs well, attentive to his own children and having their respect. For if someone is unable to handle his own affairs, how can he take care of God's church? He must not be a new believer, lest the position go to his head and the Devil trip him up. Outsiders must think well of him, or else the Devil will figure out a way to lure him into his trap.

We love because he first loved us.

So here's what I want you to do. When you gather for worship, each one of you be prepared with something that will be useful for all: Sing a hymn, teach a lesson, tell a story, lead a prayer, provide an insight. If prayers are offered in tongues, two or three's the limit, and then only if someone is present who can interpret what you're saying. Otherwise, keep it between God and yourself. And no more than two or three speakers at a meeting, with the rest of you listening and taking it to heart. Take your turn, no one person taking over. Then each speaker gets a chance to say something special from God, and you all learn from each other. If you choose to speak, you're also responsible for how and when you speak. When we worship the right way, God doesn't stir us up into confusion; he brings us into harmony. This goes for all the churches—no exceptions.

Anyone who sets himself up as "religious" by talking a good game is self-deceived. This kind of religion is hot air and only hot air. Real religion, the kind that passes muster before God the Father, is this: Reach out to the homeless and loveless in their plight, and guard against corruption from the godless world.

SELF EVALUATION TIME

Now, that we see how the and why the church was built now ask yourself is our service truly as it should be in the church.

can only share my experiences but I pray me being honest it will help you to be onest with yourself. I know, I went to church just because I was doing it as a hild. My grandfather took me to church where he served as a Sunday School eacher. I did like to go to church as we had a day care center in there, we often ate ood and there were some nice people there.

Once I was an adult I went from time to time but honestly had this attitude lat I did not need to go to church. I was a good person. I helped people when ley needed me to. I knew who God and Jesus was.

Turns out I was spiritually blind. I did not have a relationship with the Lord leaning, I went to in the church building but that was it. I would usually, not pay ttention to the message being delivered. I was often talking to someone that was round me. I am always honest about an issue I had with the preachers always aying the same ole thing every time I went to church. Turns out that was the best ling I could've heard and that was the actual Gospel of Jesus Christ. Jesus died, esus was buried, Jesus got out the grave in 3 days!

s I stated I gave my life to Christ September 2011 and never looked back. lthough my journey haven't been the easiest it sure isn't the worst. I am grateful or the opportunity to wake of each day as it is a blessing from God.

I have had visions from God since I was a little girl but had no idea what as really going on until I accepted Christ wholeheartedly, meaning I gave up my ay of thinking and believing and gave into the Holy Spirit as I was spoken to and uided. I must be honest accepting the call to preach the Word of God was the cariest things I could of done. It was scary because the intimate relationship with le Lord is such an awesome experience that it is scary knowing the power of God nd the love He has for little ole me is unspeakably rewarding in itself.

I must also be honest that positioning from a blessed member of the Body to eing a blessed member on the front line of the battlefield is very tough. I have a ery strong personality and it is often confused with arrogance or a know it all. I m honestly the complete opposite. I am a very quiet person that loves to sit and observe and learn but when there is something I do not agree with or feel strongly about, I am not at all afraid to voice and stand up for it. I am a very defensive person when it comes to defending those that are not as quick to speak up when they are not being treated fairly. My standing up for what's right is not limited to anyone in position if things are not right.

I am in ministry and it is male dominated and I really get things stirred up being a woman that is not afraid to call out injustice. I am looked at as a trouble maker or out of order when in fact I know that I am led by the Holy Spirit. It is just so accepted by people to sit back and allow wrongs over take what's right when it comes to leadership in the church.

This is another reason that God guided me to write this book in the format that it is. It is scripture based with a time out for each of us to truly look at our own behaviors and correct what's in error and increase in what is good.

We all have gifts and talents blessed by God. It is too often that the leaders in the churches are so wrapped up in themselves and intimidated by others that they are in error and the churches are not moving forward as they should. Too many pastors are all about themselves and using the church as a financial gain for themselves and their families that they've lost focus on what it truly is they are their for. Too often pastors get so caught up in their own agendas they run the churches down, run members away and fault others as the problems when in fact it is their behaviors that cause the dark cloud over the house of worship they have been blessed to oversee. I am able to say this from experience from being on this side of the church and I must say just as there are many that do not care for me I too do not care for their actions as it is not a good reflection on the body of Christ.

Too often we as members of the Body of Christ do not look at what we consider small things that doesn't hurt, very much does hurt the church. Some may feel that they have not murdered anyone or cheated on their spouse, they are not homosexual and things of this nature. Take the time to really look at Christ behaviors. If you only use the church for your financial benefit but don't do anything to really help or care for the people in the church, you are a thief. If you go to church to pick up men or women for sex just because you know many trust you because you are in church all the time, you are a liar and a whore (male and female). When you go just to see what's going on to gossip, you too are a hypocrite.

Just think about all these things we are witnessing now. With cameras everywhere and social media we see more than we would like too. People are defiling the house of worship with sex acts in them both heterosexual and homosexual, just no respect for the Lords house. I just saw a video of a married pastor performing oral sex on a woman. A Pastors son was having sex with a man inside of the sanctuary. It doesn't matter if you are a pastor or not this is a dark cloud being placed on the church and this is why people would rather be in the streets with hanging out than coming in a church full of hypocrites. One more thing for those in leadership that is always talking about money from the pulpit. If you are leading the people in a true Christ like manner, the people with take care of the church house. When the membership and funds are low, it is a reflection of your leadership and it is time for you to accept that and either step away because your heart is not truly committed or Make a true and sincere turnaround and be about Gods business and not your own selfish business.

For the members that sit back and complain behind closed doors but do not stand up for Gods business you are just as guilty as the ones you sit back and watch do these things but too afraid to loose what little they have to offer you. There is a way to handle things, but too often we just accept the wrong knowing nothing is right about what's happening.

List things I can do better according to the scriptures I read in this chapter

_____
_____
_____
_____
_____
_____

List of things I am not proud about that I am going to ask god to help me correct

_____
_____
_____
_____
_____
_____

Things that I am thankful to say I do well to build up the body of Christ

_____
_____
_____
_____
_____
_____

Chapter Six: Our Dealings In Our Personal Homes

We love because he first loved us.

When Jesus had completed these teachings, he left Galilee and crossed the region of Judea on the other side of the Jordan. Great crowds followed him there, and he healed them.

One day the Pharisees were badgering him: "Is it legal for a man to divorce his wife for any reason?"

He answered, "Haven't you read in your Bible that the Creator originally made man and woman for each other, male and female? And because of this, a man leaves father and mother and is firmly bonded to his wife, becoming one flesh—no longer two bodies but one. Because God created this organic union of the two sexes, no one should desecrate his art by cutting them apart."

They shot back in rebuttal, "If that's so, why did Moses give instructions for divorce papers and divorce procedures?"

Jesus said, "Moses provided for divorce as a concession to your hard heartedness, but it is not part of God's original plan. I'm holding you to the original plan, and holding you liable for adultery if you divorce your faithful wife and then marry someone else. I make an exception in cases where the spouse has committed adultery."

Jesus' disciples objected, "If those are the terms of marriage, we're stuck. Why get married?"

But Jesus said, "Not everyone is mature enough to live a married life. It requires a certain aptitude and grace. Marriage isn't for everyone. Some, from birth seemingly, never give marriage a thought. Others never get asked—or accepted. And some decide not to get married for kingdom reasons. But if you're capable of growing into the largeness of marriage, do it.

What Pollutes Your Life

After that, Pharisees and religion scholars came to Jesus all the way from Jerusalem, criticizing, "Why do your disciples play fast and loose with the rules?"

But Jesus put it right back on them. "Why do you use your rules to play fast and loose with God's commands? God clearly says, 'Respect your father and mother,' and, 'Anyone denouncing father or mother should be killed.' But you weasel *around that by saying, 'Whoever wants to, can say to father and mother, What I owed to you I've given to God.' That can hardly be called respecting a parent. You cancel God's command by your rules. Frauds! Isaiah's prophecy of you hit the bull's-eye:*

These people make a big show of saying the right thing, but their heart isn't in it. They act like they're worshiping me, but they don't mean it. They just use me as a cover for teaching whatever suits their fancy."

Children, obey your parents in everything, for this pleases the Lord.

SELF EVALUATION TIME

Oh what we do in our homes are so important. I often say I am who I am because that is just the truth. I can feel good about this because I am a good wife to my husband, of course we all can be better in all that we do. I take pride in being married to my husband. Has it always been easy, no baby no! Marriage is all about selflessness, communication, compromise, giving and receiving. All marriages goes through ups and downs. Of course its easier when you are in your uplifting times but they are truly defined through the not so good times. These days so many think it is all about me and could care less about the other person. My husband told me once both of us cant wear the pants in the marriage. That really pissed me off but I did hear him because I am so independent because of my personality I just never looked for anyone to be in control over me rather than understanding he wanted to work with me not against me. Make no mistakes about it there were things about him that needed to change as well and yes we both realize that we are better together than apart and most definitely worth the compromise to make the other feel the love and desire of being together.

It is so easy to walk away from a marriage or any relationship but when you really look it doesn't get any easier because the same problems keep coming up in every relationship you enter because you have not accepted the issues you bring with you. When we are not at our full level of completeness we can not bring happiness with another. We must find out who we are and be happy and in good standings with ourselves or we have nothing to offer anyone else except the misery that is truly deep down within ourselves.

This holds truth to our parenting as well. When we are not where we need to be as a person, we pass the cycle of behaviors on to our children. Many times we how our anger that is deep within how we raise our children. Often times we want to be more involved with a sexual partner and not giving what we should to our children. We may want to hang out with our friends and not spending the quality time with our spouses. How we talk to one another is another thing that brings down the family. When there is resentment or unresolved issues you haven't worked through, you will never get back on track in the relationships in our home. You must talk about things, not just hold them in and bring them up during an argument months to a year later and the other one doesn't even know what you are talking about or you feel like they've been fake because they've been

37

feeling this way all along but acting like its been ok, that makes you feel like you are sleeping with the enemy and that is not a good place to be in a relationship.

Another thing you must not base a relationship on things material and or financial. There are things that will always happen. People lose jobs, get sick, and so on. If you are building your home life according to nice things and nice bank accounts you have already lost. If it is not love and relationship building your are working on you may as well remain alone because that's where you will surely end up.

Children listen to your parents and be there for them when they need you most. If we are blessed to have our parents when they get to a place they get older and weaker needing you to take care of them. DO IT WITH NO STRINGS ATTACHED, NOT LOOKING FOR ANYTHING IN RETURN EXCEPT THE NEED TO WANT TO GIVE TO THEM WHAT THEY HAVE GIVEN TO YOU WHEN YOU COULD NOT DO FOR YOURSELF.

The hardest thing for me was the deaths of my beloved Grandparents that raised me. The good thing about it is they both died knowing I loved them for them and not what they had to offer me. One thing that keeps me going on with pride is they trusted me with everything including the trust that I would care for the other once the other was gone, if they did not go together. It was a true sacrifice for me to stay on the road from one state to another but it is something that I would do all over again if I had the chance.

See we as people have to look at our motives in the things we do. Yes, it is a very sad truth that there are some that only look at their parents as cash and what they have to offer them, not out of genuine love. I am sure some may say, people are not that heartless but I am hear to tell you oh yes there are plenty of them out here like this. Being in Healthcare and personal experiences of my own allows me to bare witness to this. I honestly feel bad for those that have these types of spirits because they will surely experience great pain when the Lord shows them their ways in His timing. People do not like to talk about the nasty things family do but it is biblical and I believe the Bible and I will never forget the first murder committed in the Bible was between brothers and that is enough for me to know being family does not mean everyone is truly for you and will not do harm to you for what ever their motives may me.

List things I can do better according to the scriptures I read in this chapter

_____
_____
_____
_____
_____
_____
_____

List of things I am not proud about that I am going to ask god to help me correct

_____
_____
_____
_____
_____
_____

Things that I am thankful to say I do well to build up the body of Christ

_____
_____
_____
_____
_____
_____

Chapter Seven: Our Dealings With One Another

Peter's Vision

There was a man named Cornelius who lived in Caesarea, captain of the Italian Guard stationed there. He was a thoroughly good man. He had led everyone in his house to live worshipfully before God, was always helping people in need, and had the habit of prayer. One day about three o'clock in the afternoon he had a vision. An angel of God, as real as his next-door neighbor, came in and said, "Cornelius."

Cornelius stared hard, wondering if he was seeing things. Then he said, "What do you want, sir?"

The angel said, "Your prayers and neighborly acts have brought you to God's attention. Here's what you are to do. Send men to Joppa to get Simon, the one everyone calls Peter. He is staying with Simon the Tanner, whose house is down by the sea."

As soon as the angel was gone, Cornelius called two servants and one particularly devout soldier from the guard. He went over with them in great detail everything that had just happened, and then sent them off to Joppa.

The next day as the three travelers were approaching the town, Peter went out on the balcony to pray. It was about noon. Peter got hungry and started thinking about lunch. While lunch was being prepared, he fell into a trance. He saw the skies open up. Something that looked like a huge blanket lowered by ropes at its four corners settled on the ground. Every kind of animal and reptile and bird you could think of was on it. Then a voice came: "Go to it, Peter—kill and eat."

Peter said, "Oh, no, Lord. I've never so much as tasted food that was not kosher. The voice came a second time: "If God says it's okay, it's okay." This happened three times, and then the blanket was pulled back up into the skies.

As Peter, puzzled, sat there trying to figure out what it all meant, the men sent by Cornelius showed up at Simon's front door. They called in, asking if there was a Simon, also called Peter, staying there. Peter, lost in thought, didn't hear them, so the Spirit whispered to him, "Three men are knocking at the door looking for you.

Get down there and go with them. Don't ask any questions. I sent them to get you."

Peter went down and said to the men, "I think I'm the man you're looking for. What's up?" They said, "Captain Cornelius, a God-fearing man well-known for his fair play—ask any Jew in this part of the country—was commanded by a holy angel to get you and bring you to his house so he could hear what you had to say." Peter invited them in and made them feel at home.

God Plays No Favorites

The next morning he got up and went with them. Some of his friends from Joppa went along. A day later they entered Caesarea. Cornelius was expecting them and had his relatives and close friends waiting with him. The minute Peter came through the door, Cornelius was up on his feet greeting him—and then down on his face worshiping him! Peter pulled him up and said, "None of that—I'm a man and only a man, no different from you."

Talking things over, they went on into the house, where Cornelius introduced Peter to everyone who had come. Peter addressed them, "You know, I'm sure that this is highly irregular. Jews just don't do this—visit and relax with people of another race. But God has just shown me that no race is better than any other. So the minute I was sent for, I came, no questions asked. But now I'd like to know why you sent for me."

Cornelius said, "Four days ago at about this time, midafternoon, I was home praying. Suddenly there was a man right in front of me, flooding the room with light. He said, 'Cornelius, your daily prayers and neighborly acts have brought you to God's attention. I want you to send to Joppa to get Simon, the one they call Peter. He's staying with Simon the Tanner down by the sea.'

So I did it—I sent for you. And you've been good enough to come. And now we're all here in God's presence, ready to listen to whatever the Master put in your heart to tell us."

Peter fairly exploded with his good news: "It's God's own truth, nothing could be plainer: God plays no favorites! It makes no difference who you are or where you're from—if you want God and are ready to do as he says, the door is open. The Message he sent to the children of Israel—that through Jesus Christ everything is being put together again—well, he's doing it everywhere, among everyone.

"You know the story of what happened in Judea. It began in Galilee after John preached a total life-change. Then Jesus arrived from Nazareth, anointed by God with the Holy Spirit, ready for action. He went through the country helping people and healing everyone who was beaten down by the Devil. He was able to do all this because God was with him.

"And we saw it, saw it all, everything he did in the land of the Jews and in Jerusalem where they killed him, hung him from a cross. But in three days God had him up, alive, and out where he could be seen. Not everyone saw him—he wasn't put on public display. Witnesses had been carefully handpicked by God beforehand—us! We were the ones, there to eat and drink with him after he came back from the dead. He commissioned us to announce this in public, to bear solemn witness that he is in fact the One whom God destined as Judge of the living and dead. But we're not alone in this. Our witness that he is the means to forgiveness of sins is backed up by the witness of all the prophets."

No sooner were these words out of Peter's mouth than the Holy Spirit came on the listeners. The believing Jews who had come with Peter couldn't believe it, couldn't believe that the gift of the Holy Spirit was poured out on "outsider" non-Jews, but there it was—they heard them speaking in tongues, heard them praising God.

Then Peter said, "Do I hear any objections to baptizing these friends with water? They've received the Holy Spirit exactly as we did." Hearing no objections, he ordered that they be baptized in the name of Jesus Christ. Then they asked Peter to stay on for a few days.

SELF EVALUATION TIME

It is so often that we do not want to help or do things for others due to our ejudices. Look at Peter telling God what he was not going to do because of his titude about Cornelius. After Peter came down off his high horse and was bedient, he had to turn around and put the others in their place just as God did m. It's just amazing how powerful our God is and how He show us so much, if e just listen and obey Him.

There is so much that affects every relationship we have according to what's eep rooted in us. Even on our jobs we expect the jobs to do everything we want or us but are not even a good employee. We have nasty attitudes but expect veryone to give us the utmost respect.

We may have deep rooted racism in us, but we attempt to convince urselves we don't because we work with the other races. Well, we may work together but do you ever take the time to self evaluate you have some very nasty ays in how you treat those that are in lower positions than you feel, those that ok differently , those that live differently.

These days although we may not agree but lets talk about homosexuality for moment. I will be the first to admit, I believe a man and woman is what defy a lationship because that's what the Word of God says and I believe it and stand on . I do also know that I am not to treat anyone differently because they are gay. I ealize being gay is what God says is wrong at the same time I do not lie to myself at I do things that are wrong as well and being gay is no worse than things I do. I an get very mean at times when people hurt me. I have the ability to curse you so ad for a few moments and ready to actually fight because I have a fight in me that something terrible when you push me too far. My point is I am wrong and no ifferent than anyone else that goes against what God says.

I am also very big on treating everyone equal. I cant stand for people to think they are better than someone because of the type of work they do. I myself m looked up on as less than those that are a Nurse by some but I know that my job what I do, it is not who I am. I laugh being in healthcare management I know ome things about some and wonder who did you buy or steal your licensee or egree from. I just encourage people to use the examples of Christ. Christ was humbled and loved everyone. People talk about immigrants, well Jesus was considered an immigrant but what a wonderful one He is and what if He was denied the way people attempt to judge others by their ethnicity. We really need to wake up before it it too late, Jesus is coming back for His people and His people are those that are genuine in their characteristics of Himself.   Please don't hear the words :I NEVER KNEW YOU; DEPART FROM ME. I am working on me too, because I am not exempt.

List things I can do better according to the scriptures I read in this chapter

_____
_____
_____
_____
_____
_____
_____

List of things I am not proud about that I am going to ask god to help me correct

_____
_____
_____
_____
_____
_____

Things that I am thankful to say I do well to build up the body of Christ

_____
_____
_____
_____
_____
_____

Chapter Eight: Our New Beginnings In The Body Of CHRIST

If I give everything I own to the poor and even go to the stake to be burned as a martyr, but I don't love, I've gotten nowhere. So, no matter what I say, what I believe, and what I do, I'm bankrupt without love.

Love never gives up.
Love cares more for others than for self.
Love doesn't want what it doesn't have.
Love doesn't strut,
Doesn't have a swelled head,
Doesn't force itself on others,
Isn't always "me first,"
Doesn't fly off the handle,
Doesn't keep score of the sins of others,
Doesn't revel when others grovel,
Takes pleasure in the flowering of truth,
Puts up with anything,
Trusts God always,
Always looks for the best,
Never looks back,
But keeps going to the end.

List things I can do better according to the scriptures I read in this chapter

_____
_____
_____
_____
_____
_____

List of things I am not proud about that I am going to ask god to help me correct

_____
_____
_____
_____
_____
_____

Things that I am thankful to say I do well to build up the body of Christ

_____
_____
_____
_____
_____
_____

Epilogue/Conclusion

I Sincerely thank you for your purchase and taking the time to read.

I do pray that after reading this small but powerful book you will take the time to truly look at you. We all have enough to work on self and not look at the next person. When we are looking at the next person, let us be working to help build up and not tear down. When people tell you something that may be hard to hear it just may be something that will help you to be more Christ like in some way. This journey is not easy as we come in contact with so many personalities and if you are like me there are so many emotions that go on within myself that drives me to take a step back.

I truly did write from my heart to help us all help one another. I spoke my truths in order to ensure you as the reader I am no different, I just have a calling upon life to stand up and stand out.

As we enter into our new beginnings of Christ like behaviors seek the Lord in Prayer to help see things that you may not be able to. Stay open as you look for God to reveal to you through what you may see, through what you may hear and through your hearts convictions. God does things in many ways but the great thing about Gods way it most certainly is the right way

I most certainly pray for you and you pray for me.

Bibliography

All scriptures were taken from the Holy Bible through the Bible Gateway site.

English Standard Version (ESV)

The Message Version (MSG)

I chose these versions as they are easier to read and comprehend as I want this book to be an easy but powerful and life changing read.

About the Author

Latasha L. Willingham is just an everyday person that works a full time career as a Food & Nutrition/Environmental Services Manager in Hospice Care. Latasha's career in Healthcare Management over 20 years beginning as a Foodservice Assistant that was responsible for Desser and beverage preparation in the Nursing Home field which led to a speedy advancement into Management.

Christ Jesus Disciple Ministries is the ministry that God call Latasha to oversee, that will focus on outreach for the community. She also has a small business that she and her husband runs selling clothing, soap and body creams and much more.

Latasha studied at The University of North Dakota Correspondence course in Dietary Management. The Author enrolled in courses studying to become a Dietitian for 2 years when an opportunity opened for her to move into the Hospice Care Field when the Lord shifted her.

As she was driving in job in September 2011 she had an experience with the Lord when she journeyed back into the House of the Lord although hesitant and afraid she knew she had works to do after years of being away. She was very nervous but determined to be obediently led in the direction God had been calling her for years. She began by teaching Sunday school, Ushering on the Usher board however no matter how much she attempted to run from the Call of God she eventually accepted and announced her calling before the people of in July of 2014 and preaching her Initial Sermon December of 2014, being Ordained October 2016.

Studied and Graduated from Brewster Theological Clinic school of Religion August 2015. Studied and Graduated from Jacksonville Theological Seminary, Revelation Message Bible College, Bachelor of Ministry May 2017.

TO

Lioness

a beautiful woman
inside and out,
God placed you in my
life and I am thankful
only Greatness to come
your way
Love ya
Tasha
AKA
BOSSChic

Made in the USA
Middletown, DE
26 August 2020